EXPLORING EARTH'S HABITATS

FOREST HABITATS
AROUND THE WORLD

M. M. Eboch

Raintree is an imprint of Capstone Global Library Limited, a company incorporated in England and Wales having its registered office at 264 Banbury Road, Oxford, OX2 7DY – Registered company number: 6695582

www.raintree.co.uk
myorders@raintree.co.uk

Edited by Gina Kammer
Designed by Julie Peters
Original illustrations © Capstone Global Library Limited 2020
Picture research by Morgan Walters
Production by Kathy McColley
Originated by Capstone Global Library Ltd
Printed and bound in India

ISBN: 978 1 4747 8579 2 (hardback)
ISBN: 978 1 4747 8586 0 (paperback)

British Library Cataloguing in Publication Data
A full catalogue record for this book is available from the British Library.

Acknowledgements
We would like to thank the following for permission to reproduce photographs: Alamy: Steve Taylor ARPS, bottom 10; Newscom: Ingo Arndt/ Minden Pictures, bottom 12, Staff/The News & Observer, bottom 28, Yingling/MCT, 15; Reuters Pictures: REUTERS GRAPHICS, 6; Science Source: Gary Hincks, bottom 5; Shutterstock: Andrei Ksenzhuk, 21, Bildagentur Zoonar GmbH, bottom 17, Brandy McKnight, bottom 8, Danita Delmont, bottom 20, Dariusz Leszczynski, top 23, dugdax, background 8-9, background 10-11, FedBul, top 25, Gabriel Ostapchuk, background 18-19, background 20-21, background 22-23, isak55, background 12, background 14-15, background 16-17, Jeff Feverston, top 13, KayaMe, (rainforest) Cover, Lillian Tveit, top right 14, Marten_House, bottom 22, miroslav chytil, bottom 16, msh11133, background 24-25, background 26-27, pisaphotography, top 19, Radachynskyi Serhii, 24, rodimov, bottom 18, sabri deniz kizil, (floral) Cover, Siarhei Dzmitryienka, background 4-5, backgorund 6-7, Smileus, background 1, 2-3, 30-31, 32, (forest) Cover, XiXinXing, (man) Cover, yelantsevv, bottom 26-27

Every effort has been made to contact copyright holders of material reproduced in this book. Any omissions will be rectified in subsequent printings if notice is given to the publisher.
All the internet addresses (URLs) given in this book were valid at the time of going to press. However, due to the dynamic nature of the internet, some addresses may have changed, or sites may have changed or ceased to exist since publication. While the author and publisher regret any inconvenience this may cause readers, no responsibility for any such changes can be accepted by either the author or the publisher.

All the internet addresses (URLs) given in this book were valid at the time of going to press. However, due to the dynamic nature of the internet, some addresses may have changed, or sites may have changed or ceased to exist since publication. While the author and publisher regret any inconvenience this may cause readers, no responsibility for any such changes can be accepted by either the author or the publisher.

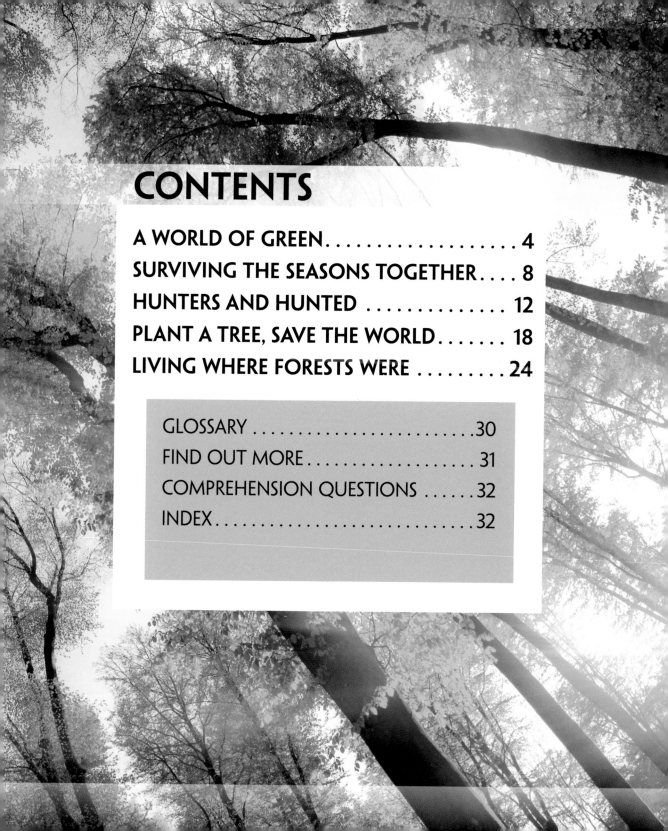

CONTENTS

CHAPTER 1

A WORLD OF GREEN

Imagine walking through a forest during autumn. Tall trees grow all around you. Their leaves are turning red, orange and yellow. Dry leaves crunch under your feet. You're in a **temperate** forest.

Forests are a type of habitat. So are deserts, grasslands, tundra and aquatic. Each type of habitat shares a **climate**. Each has animals and plants that can live there. And each habitat is important to people and our planet.

Temperate forests have a lot to offer people. Forest soil is good for growing food. Trees provide wood for building and making many products.

TEMPERATE FORESTS

Temperate forests are one of the three main types of forests in the forest habitat. Tropical forests stay hot and green all year. Boreal forests have long winters and short, cool summers. However, a temperate forest is sometimes hot and sometimes cold. Temperate forests aren't found near the cold poles or the hot equator. They flourish in the temperate zone between those two regions.

FACT BOX

Forests cover about 30 per cent of Earth's land.

Forest habitats around the world

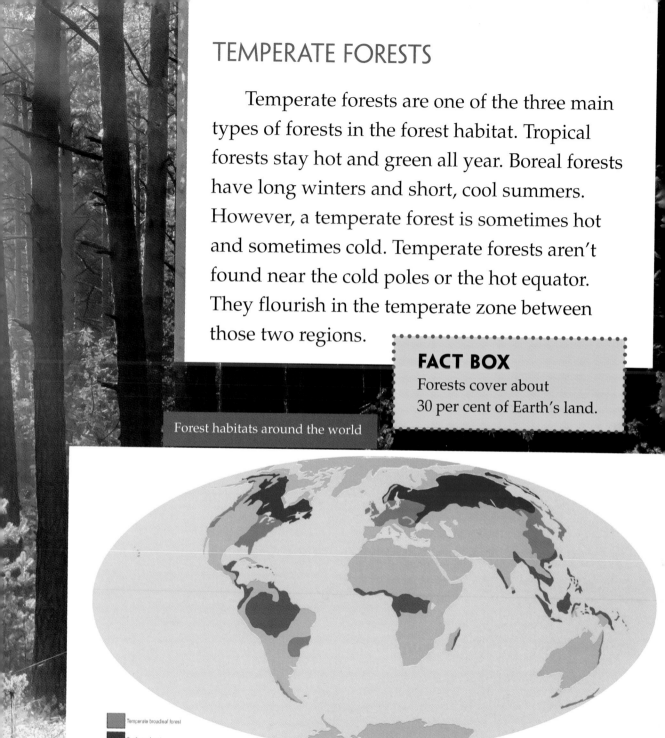

Temperate broadleaf forest

Coniferous forest

Tropical rainforest

climate usual weather conditions in a place
temperate having mild weather without very hot or very cold temperatures

5

THE FOUR SEASONS

A temperate forest has four separate seasons. In spring, the temperature rises. In some temperate forests, the **precipitation** levels also increase. Young leaves and flowers appear. Plants grow most during the heat of summer. Leaves capture sunlight to make food. In autumn, temperatures drop. Precipitation can also decrease in some areas. Leaves change colour. They dry up and fall from the trees. Winter may bring snow and freezing temperatures.

The forest habitat used to cover half of Earth's land. Around the world, people cut down forests to use the trees and farm the rich soil. Forested land has shrunk by 20 per cent. Today, a quarter of what's left is temperate forest.

precipitation moisture that lands on the ground, including rain, snow, mist or fog

The Eastern Deciduous Forest used to cover much of the eastern United States. It stretches from southern Canada to Florida. Parts go as far west as Texas and Minnesota. However, it's no longer one big forest. When European settlers arrived, people cleared the forest to make room for towns and farms. They cut down trees for firewood and building material. They built dams along rivers. Mills used the water's power to grind grain or cut logs. Only about 0.1 per cent of this forest has not been changed by humans.

DECLINING FOREST COVER

DEFORESTATION INDEX
Data evaluated for forest cover between 2005-2010

Risk level:

◼ Extreme ◼ High ◼ Medium ◼ Low ◼ No data

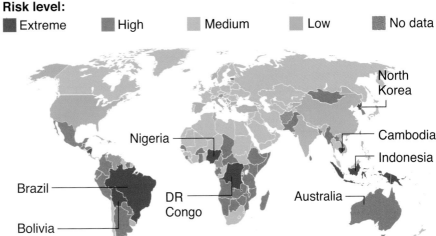

North Korea

Cambodia

Indonesia

Nigeria

Brazil

DR Congo

Australia

Bolivia

Tropical forests are one of the most common areas where trees are cut down.

CHAPTER 2

SURVIVING THE SEASONS TOGETHER

Like people, plants and animals **adapt** to the habitats where they live. In temperate forests, many plants must withstand cold winters. **Deciduous** trees such as oak, elm, ash and beech drop their leaves during autumn. This helps the tree conserve its energy during winter. The forest floor is covered with dead leaves. Snails, earthworms, flies and beetles help to break down dead leaves. The leaves then become food for the forest.

An earthworm

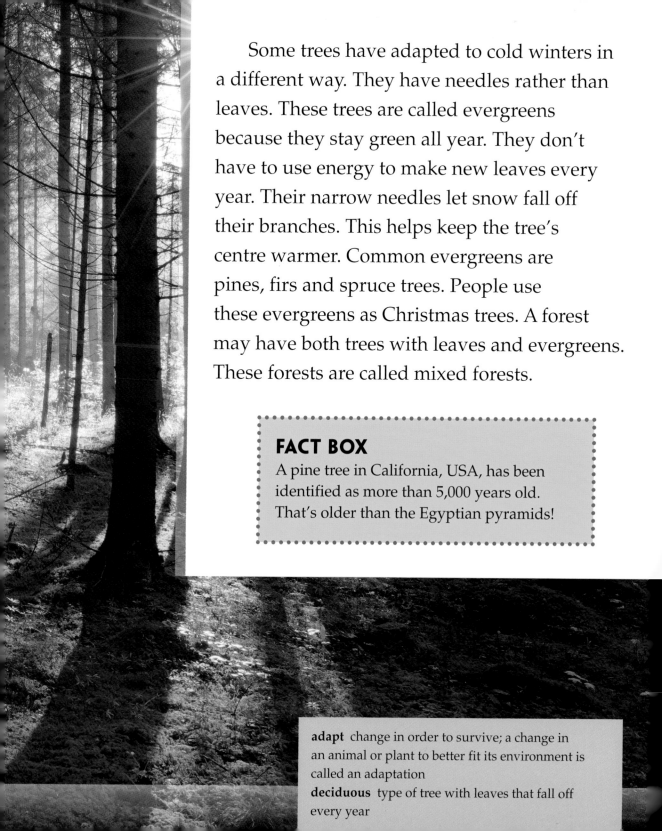

Some trees have adapted to cold winters in a different way. They have needles rather than leaves. These trees are called evergreens because they stay green all year. They don't have to use energy to make new leaves every year. Their narrow needles let snow fall off their branches. This helps keep the tree's centre warmer. Common evergreens are pines, firs and spruce trees. People use these evergreens as Christmas trees. A forest may have both trees with leaves and evergreens. These forests are called mixed forests.

FACT BOX

A pine tree in California, USA, has been identified as more than 5,000 years old. That's older than the Egyptian pyramids!

adapt change in order to survive; a change in an animal or plant to better fit its environment is called an adaptation

deciduous type of tree with leaves that fall off every year

Oak trees may live for centuries because they grow very slowly. The slow growth helps them survive low light and dry seasons. In the UK, legend says that the outlaw hero Robin Hood lived in Sherwood Forest. Today, Sherwood Forest has more than 900 big oak trees. One of Sherwood Forest's oaks may be 1,000 years old. The stories say this massive oak was a meeting place for Robin Hood and his friends.

A large oak tree in Sherwood Forest

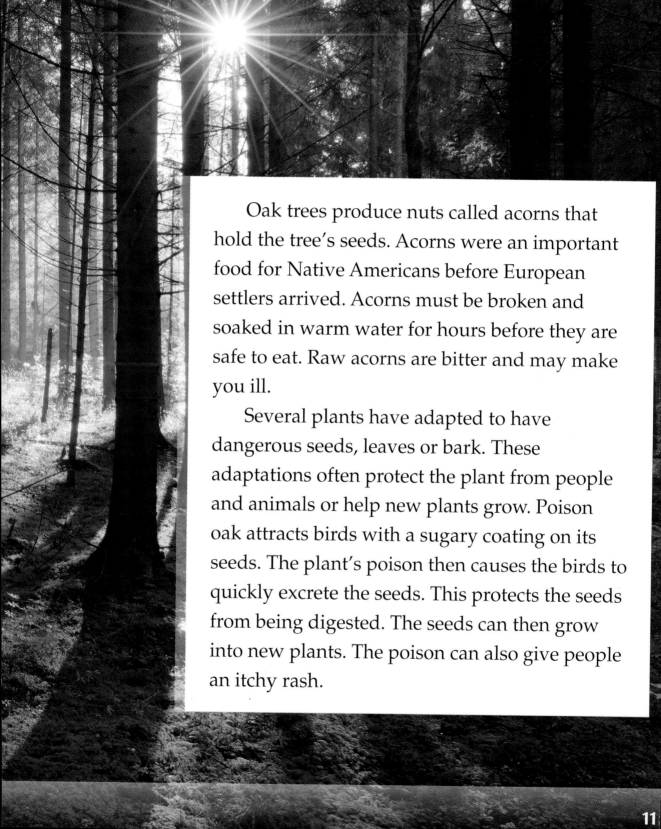

Oak trees produce nuts called acorns that hold the tree's seeds. Acorns were an important food for Native Americans before European settlers arrived. Acorns must be broken and soaked in warm water for hours before they are safe to eat. Raw acorns are bitter and may make you ill.

Several plants have adapted to have dangerous seeds, leaves or bark. These adaptations often protect the plant from people and animals or help new plants grow. Poison oak attracts birds with a sugary coating on its seeds. The plant's poison then causes the birds to quickly excrete the seeds. This protects the seeds from being digested. The seeds can then grow into new plants. The poison can also give people an itchy rash.

CHAPTER 3

HUNTERS
AND HUNTED

Temperate forests are home to deer, foxes, raccoons, skunks, rabbits and birds. All these animals must deal with warm summers and cold winters. Some, including butterflies and some birds, **migrate** to avoid winter. Some animals hide food for later. Squirrels gather nuts in autumn. They store them to eat in winter, when food is hard to find. Other animals **hibernate**. Black bears, toads, frogs, snakes and turtles rest in winter so that they don't need to try and find food.

A mother black bear and her cub hibernate in the winter.

A doe in winter

Though deer don't hibernate, they are less active in winter. They may not move for several days, living off their stored fat. Deer prepare for winter by growing thick, heavy coats. Their winter coat is darker, so it absorbs more sunlight for warmth. A deer's skin produces oil, which helps its fur stay dry in the snow.

hibernate go into a resting state over the winter, as if in a deep sleep
migrate travel from one area to another on a regular basis

Grey wolves have adapted to hunt deer in winter. The wolves have strong jaws for killing and eating large animals. Wolves also have thick coats to protect them from the cold. They have good hearing and night vision. Their sense of smell is 100 times better than a human's.

Grey wolves

People often fear wolves, even though they rarely harm humans. Hunters don't want wolves to kill game animals such as deer. Farmers worry that wolves will kill farm animals. Wolves once roamed throughout North American forests. Then people began hunting wolves. In many areas, wolves were wiped out. Only a small population was left in the northern Midwest by the mid-1900s. In 1973, laws began protecting wolves. Their numbers grew, but far fewer wolves live now than in the past.

Today many of the laws protecting wolves have ended. More wolves are being killed again.

AMERICAN GREY WOLF DISTRIBUTION

Wolf distribution

■ Current range ▢ Historic range

Western Great Lakes population

Wash.

Mont.

Ore.

Northern Rocky Mountain population

Idaho

Wyo.

Minn.

Wis.

Mich.

Ariz.

N.M.

Mexican wolf population

Grey wolf
Canis lupus

Grey wolf populations began to climb once again after they were listed as endangered in the 1970s.

KEEPING THE BALANCE

People still fear wolves. But wolves have a valuable role in nature. They're a **keystone species**, which means that they are very important to their environment. Wolves help control the numbers of other animals. Without wolves, animal populations can get out of control.

Grey wolves in winter

Wolves, bears and mountain lions used to control the deer population. Today many of these large predators have disappeared. The deer population has greatly increased. More deer live in North America today than ever before. Too many deer can harm a forest. Deer don't hibernate in winter. They eat anything they can find, including new buds on trees. They eat plants that other animals, such as birds, need. Deer can also spread diseases to people.

People can help keep animal species in balance. One way is to let large animals such as wolves hunt freely. Hunting laws can also help manage animal numbers.

American red wolves

FACT BOX
Wolves communicate by howling. A pack may howl together to say, "This is our territory."

keystone species species so important that losing it would affect other species

CHAPTER 4

PLANT A TREE, SAVE THE WORLD

Forests benefit people in many ways. Forests provide **timber**. Timber can be made into writing paper, toilet paper, paper towels and much more. Forests provide food, too. Some people hunt forest animals, such as pheasant or deer. Temperate forests also have many nuts and berries. Forest mushrooms can be poisonous, but some types are a good source of food.

timber wood from trees used for building and making things

People often gather in parks to get closer to nature.

Trees and plants provide another very important thing – oxygen. Oxygen is the most important part of the air we breathe. Forests near roads reduce the noise and pollution from cars. Cleaner air means healthier people. Forests in city parks make the city prettier and attract visitors. The trees provide shade that helps keep cities cooler in summer.

Temperate forests also provide homes to many animals. New species of plants and animals are found every year.

Scientists announced a new species of hemlock tree in 2017. It's found only in temperate forests in Korea. Hemlocks are homes for some insects and birds. In the eastern United States, an insect from Japan is killing the hemlocks. However, the insects don't kill the Korean trees. Scientists are studying the Korean hemlocks to learn how they might be able to save the American hemlock trees.

A hemlock grove

Other new species might be good for food or have other benefits to humans. Many plants and animals are used in medicines, so a new species could save lives. Cutting down a forest could wipe out a new species before anyone finds it.

Young puffball mushrooms can be safe to eat, but many types are deadly. Only mushroom experts should gather wild mushrooms.

THE LOST FOREST

Some forests have been completely cut down. This process is known as clear-cutting. The loss of forests is called **deforestation**. Cleared land may be needed for growing crops or grazing farm animals. People may want to use the timber. However, deforestation causes problems. The trees that make oxygen are being cut down. Animals lose their homes. Rain washes away the exposed soil. Soil can flow into rivers and harm fish. Yet, we need trees for building and making paper products.

An area of pine trees is cut down in Scotland

deforestation cutting down of forests

Forests can be thinned without clear-cutting. Trees can be removed when they are old and no longer healthy. This leaves room for younger trees to grow. The forest continues, and we keep benefiting from it.

Cut logs are ready to be picked up and taken out of the forest

CHAPTER 5

LIVING WHERE FORESTS WERE

Was your town or city once a forest?

Early people lived by hunting and gathering wild foods. Forests were ideal homes for hunter-gatherers. It isn't too hot or too cold. The land is good for growing food. Rainfall and streams provide water.

However, actually living in a forest is challenging. The thick groups of trees make it hard to build houses, plant crops or travel. People often cut down the trees to clear land. Then they build houses, plant crops and build towns. Over time, towns grow into cities. Yet some people manage to live in forests as they are. They might live in small cabins far from towns. They may hunt and gather food from the forest or plant their own crops.

A cabin home in the woods

Only stumps are left after trees are cleared in an area of forest.

There are still many forests in the UK, but they are changing. When trees are cut down for logging, different types of trees may replace them. The changing forest might not be as healthy. It might not have the same animals and plants. When forests appear in smaller patches, wild animals have less room to move freely.

CHANGING CLIMATE

Pollution also affects forests. High levels of pollution stunt or stop plant growth. **Climate change** affects temperature, rainfall and weather. An area may become too hot or too dry for the plants and animals that live there. Some species may move to new areas. Other plants and animals may die out as the climate warms.

A warmer climate can also result in more storms and fires that damage forests. Every year wildfires destroy millions of acres of forests across Earth. Climate change may bring more and deadlier wildfires.

climate change significant change in Earth's climate over a period of time

Climate change also affects insects. Insects are a key part of the forest habitat. They help plants make seeds. But not all insects are good for forests. Some insects weaken or kill trees. Beetles and moths have killed huge patches of forest. Climate change causes higher temperatures. This change lets some insects grow more quickly and move into new areas.

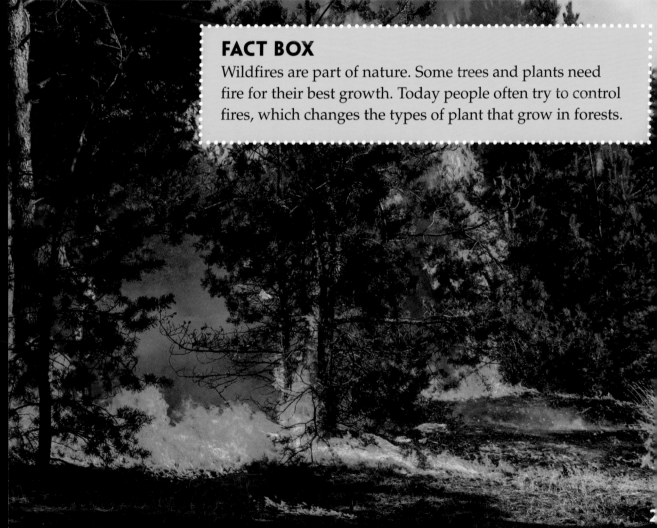

FACT BOX

Wildfires are part of nature. Some trees and plants need fire for their best growth. Today people often try to control fires, which changes the types of plant that grow in forests.

Temperature changes can also encourage the growth of **invasive species**. These plants or animals are new to an area. The **native species** may not be able to compete. Invasive species can take over, while native species die out. The Japanese insect killing hemlock trees, the hemlock woolly adelgid, is an invasive species.

Controlling a tree killer

The hemlock woolly adelgid, an exotic pest, is killing two species of hemlock, the eastern and Carolina, both in the United States.

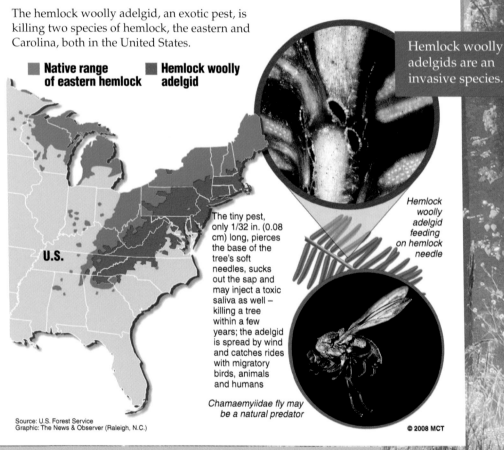

■ **Native range of eastern hemlock**   ■ **Hemlock woolly adelgid**

Hemlock woolly adelgids are an invasive species.

Hemlock woolly adelgid feeding on hemlock needle

U.S.

The tiny pest, only 1/32 in. (0.08 cm) long, pierces the base of the tree's soft needles, sucks out the sap and may inject a toxic saliva as well – killing a tree within a few years; the adelgid is spread by wind and catches rides with migratory birds, animals and humans

Chamaemyiidae fly may be a natural predator

Source: U.S. Forest Service
Graphic: The News & Observer (Raleigh, N.C.)

© 2008 MCT

invasive species species new to an area, which may spread easily and cause harm
native species species that lives and grows naturally in a particular region without the help of humans

SAVING THE FORESTS

There is hope for forests. They can grow back if given the chance, but this process takes many years. People can help by planting new trees. Iceland lost almost all of its forests. Now people in Iceland are planting about 3 million new trees every year. In the UK, the government is planning to plant a new forest across the country. It should one day be a ribbon of 50 million new trees. Robin Hood would be happy!

Across the world, conservation groups are hoping to replace deforestation with **reforestation**. That means more trees for healthy forests. Healthy forests help people and the planet stay healthy. That's good for every species.

FACT BOX

What can you do? Fighting climate change is a good way to protect every habitat. You can help. Think "reduce, reuse, recycle". Reduce what you use by buying less. Get used clothes and toys from a charity shop. Use things for as long as you can. When you can no longer use something, recycle it.

Take extra care with paper products. Most paper comes from trees. You can buy recycled paper. Use both sides of a piece of paper, and then recycle it. Avoid paper plates, cups and napkins that get thrown away. Instead, buy products you can use again.

reforestation process of planting trees where original trees were cut down

GLOSSARY

adapt change in order to survive; a change in an animal or plant to better fit its environment is called an adaptation

climate usual weather conditions in a place

climate change significant change in Earth's climate over a period of time

deciduous type of tree with leaves that fall off every year

deforestation cutting down of forests

hibernate go into a resting state over the winter, as if in a deep sleep

invasive species species new to an area, which may spread easily and cause harm

keystone species species so important that losing it would hurt other species

migrate travel from one area to another on a regular basis

native species species that lives and grows naturally in a particular region without the help of humans

precipitation moisture that lands on the ground, including rain, snow, mist or fog

reforestation process of planting trees where original trees were cut down

temperate having mild weather without very hot or very cold temperatures

timber wood from trees used for building and making things

FIND OUT MORE

BOOKS

Forests (Let's Explore Britain), James Nixon (Raintree, 2018)

Humans and Other Life On Earth (Humans and Our Planet),
Ava Sawyer (Raintree, 2018)

Living Earth: Exploring Life on Earth with Science Projects
(Discover Earth Science), Suzanne Garbe (Raintree, 2016)

WEBSITES

bbc.co.uk/bitesize/clips/topics/z849q6f/articles/zvsp92p
Watch a short film to discover more about habitats, their climates, landscapes and the wildlife that live in them.

dkfindout.com/uk/search/forest
Find out more about forest habitats and how to protect them.

COMPREHENSION QUESTIONS

1. Plants and animals can help humans in many ways. Is that a good reason to protect nature? Are there other reasons? Which is most important?
2. Many people are afraid of wolves. They kill a small number of farm animals each year. Should wolves be killed to protect people and farm animals? Or should wolves be protected by law? Why?
3. Climate change is affecting where plants and animals can live. Invasive species are killing off some native species. How important is it to keep things the same? Should we simply let these changes happen? Explain your answer.

INDEX